From Hell To Heaven
The Journey

by
Alan Haven

251-367-5457
Alan
P.O. Box 1490
E. Catawpa, MS
39552

Copyright © July 30, 2012
All rights reserved. No part of this book may be reproduced, scanned, or distributed in any printed or electronic form without permission.
First Edition: July 2012
Printed in the United States of America
ISBN: -9781620305010-

Table of Contents

The Beginning	7
How Do I Get Rid of Anger	39
Pride	61
Establishing Guidelines in Using the Bible	79
Finding Peace over Hell	91
External Peace vs. Internal Peace	102
Vision for the Future	119

Foreword

This real life story of a six-year-old boy's journey from the brink of death and the struggle that ensues is a thought provoking story that every adult should read and pass on its life's lessons to every child.

It will bring tears at times, smiles at other times, as he walks you through his emotional battles with others, as well as himself.

You will feel his struggle as he prays to God for help while at the same time being so angry with Him.

This struggle is brought to life on the pages of this book. It brings to light so many of the struggles we all face and how to overcome if we are to have a happy, productive life.

The author lays out instructions that seem so simple, yet brings great depth of understanding of ourselves.

This book is a must read if you are seeking for peace, contentment, and happiness in your life.

M. N. Farmer Thb, MRE, DD

Foreword

From Hell to Heaven is the true story of a terrible tragedy in a young life that begins a journey through almost unimaginable pain, suffering, anger, physical and emotional hurt, and healing that few of us will ever experience. The author's journey is that of struggle to heal body, mind, and spirit, searching for a higher purpose than the bonds of his burn-scarred body dictate. This true story takes us through his growing-up years in a very personal quest for meaning and purpose.

His journey literally takes him from the fiery pains of his own personal hell to the very real gift of Heaven through God's glorious salvation. This is a book to be read again and again for that wonderful kernel of truth—no matter what our personal, painful journey may be or may have been—that God is real, His saving grace is real, and that even from that past, terrible journey we can find peace with our Lord.

C. S. Norwood, MS
Master's Degree in Counseling

From the Author

In writing this book, one of the objectives has been to produce something that has the overall effect of being uplifting. In order to work toward this end, I have only related stories that I hope will stay focused on and not drift from the concern of a timely ending.

Sincerely,
Alan Haven

Send all correspondence to:

Haven
P.O. Box 1490
Escatawpa, MS 39552

Chapter 1

The Beginning

In 1960, there was a carefree, energetic, 6-year-old boy who lived in a small country town in the southern part of the United States. In those days it was quiet and laid back in a way that is hard to find in our fast paced society today. Fatefully, this young boy would soon discover that even in a peaceful place such as the one in which he lived, tragedy could occur in a moment that would forever change the course of his life. I was that boy, and this is my story.

In the area in which I grew up, life was slow and enjoyable. My family and I lived a quiet, simple life in our poor, rural community. My mother worked a garden, growing and canning food for the family. She also helped our neighbors with food from our garden. My father worked doing mechanical work in the factories. My brothers and sisters and I played in the woods for hours or enjoyed fishing at the river. We rode our bikes and played games with the neighborhood kids for hours on end. Sometimes when mother needed something from the store, we would walk into town for her. The store was about a mile from our house. This may sound strange, but we did not have the same worries when I was a boy as we do now. The people in our community looked out for each other. We knew every family in our community and could even recognize a different car when it came through town. This provided a safe environment for us to grow up in.

When we went into town, we would sometimes stop in at the store across the railroad tracks. It was owned by two elderly ladies who lived in the back. I loved their store, because they had the best bologna sandwiches that I had ever tasted. They made homemade bread freshly sliced, along with freshly sliced bologna and hoop cheese that they kept on the counter. I have very pleasant memories of this time in my life.

    The population of our town was very small. There were nearly 200 people in our community. It was so small in fact that it took not only all the children in our community but also those in a community nearby to fill a school bus for the ride to school. There was no freeway and no interstate in our area. There were no fire engines or ambulances. We only had a few deputy sheriffs to cover the entire county. Although a wonderful place to live, our community was not equipped to handle emergencies. Tragically, I would soon discover, even at my young age, just how ill-equipped our little town really was.

    In the winter of 1960, I turned 6 years old, doing everything a normal 6-year-old would do. I had just started the first grade, and it was fun. I was out for Christmas break and was looking forward to a very relaxing two-week vacation. While I enjoyed school, it was nice to be at home and sleeping in. Often, I was still in bed when the rest of the family was already up and about starting their day. On a morning just like this, I had slept in a little later than my brothers and sisters. I got out of bed, pulled on my blue jeans, and left on my flannel pajama top. I was hungry, so I went to find something to eat. My mother had already cooked breakfast for the rest of the family. I had slept in and missed it. I decided that I wanted some toast.

      I asked my mother if I could use the stove to make toast. She told me no. I was getting hungrier, so I kept asking her until she told me yes. She was not overly concerned, because she was only 20 feet away. Also, it was an electric stove. There was not really much that could happen.

      We did not realize at the time, but the flannel material that my pajama top was made of was not sprayed with flame retardant. The textile industry was later taken to court over this type of material, but my mother had no way of knowing that. She did not realize the danger that lay in my request.

      In 1953, Congress had enacted the Flammable Fabrics Act, which was amended in 1967 because of the ineffectiveness of the law. How well that flammable fabric and carpets are handled today is still in question. Many textile manufacturing processes have since moved to other countries in order to work with different guidelines and to save money, of course. It is my hope that no one suffers burns, especially because of "inexpensive" processes for clothing manufacturing.

As soon as mother said yes, I began making my toast. I pulled out the bread and got it ready to put on the stove. At 6 years of age, I was still relatively short at this time. I was not tall enough to reach the stove without assistance, so I pulled up a chair and climbed on the seat to help me get to the burner. I put my toast on the stove, waiting for it to finish. I don't remember now, but I often wonder what the last casual thoughts were that went through my mind before the flames engulfed me. Was I thinking about what game I could play after I finished breakfast or if I would go outside today? I just don't remember, but I know that I was not prepared for what would happen in the next few moments.

My toast was ready to eat, so I took it off the eye of the stove. Then I leaned over the stove to turn off the burner. I was still standing in the chair. While I was reaching, the bottom of my pajama top grazed the eye of the stove. While there was no open flame on the stove, the brushed flannel of my pajamas burst into flames like it had been soaked in kerosine.

I didn't know what to do. I was not prepared to handle this. My school had not taught the "golden rule" for accidental fire: to stop, drop, and roll. This was not a concept that was widely taught anywhere to my knowledge in 1960. Therefore, this was a foreign concept to me. I began to slap the flames with my hands, becoming more and more terrified by the second. With every blow I made to the flame, it seemed to spread. I couldn't stop the flames. I jumped from the chair and began to scream. I ran in all directions frantically, but this only accelerated the flames. I was so scared.

My mother heard my screams. She grabbed a coat to extinguish the flames, but in my panic all I could do was run. I was so scared that I could not think. I did not go to my mother. I continued to run, thinking that the running would extinguish the flames that were engulfing my body. My mother finally chased me down. She used the coat that she had grabbed and smothered the flames. At this point though, the damage had already been done.

When she pulled the coat off to survey the damage, 55% of my body had been ravaged by the flames. My skin was gone. The muscles and tendons on parts of my body were exposed without any covering. I lay there in agony while my mother gathered her strength and burst into action. My father was at work, and we had no way of reaching him right away. She called our neighbors, an elderly couple, and asked them for a ride to the hospital. She did not wait for the ambulance. It would have taken them over an hour to get to our home. My mother knew this might have been too late for me to survive. She could not take that chance. My older sister stayed at home with my brothers and sister while we made our way to the emergency room.

The ride to the hospital was agonizingly slow. There was no freeway to take, and we lived on country roads. The car was old, and the tires were dry rotted and fragile. The old man was afraid to drive fast. Every second seemed to tick by with excruciating slowness. Mother was afraid that with every passing moment, my chances of survival were quickly dwindling away. She prayed while holding me in her arms, hoping that by some miracle I would live.

    I lay still in my mother's arms and faded in and out of consciousness while she wiped my head with a moist cloth and whispered soothing words to try to calm my fear. The time of that long trip to the hospital seemed suspended in time. I felt heat and some type of numbness which in all likelihood was my body going into shock. I welcomed this feeling of numbness, because this was not as bad compared to the excruciating pain coming from my seared flesh.

    Finally, after what seemed like an eternity, we arrived at the hospital. Our elderly neighbor pulled slowly into the hospital parking lot. Immediately, as the car came to a stop, my mother, clutching me in her arms, raced towards emergency room doors. There was a nurse just outside the doors taking a break. When she realized what was happening, she ran through the emergency room doors ahead of us telling the other hospital staff we were coming.

    They were ready for us as soon we came through the doors. I remember doctors and nurses rushing around for different attachments that were being fastened to a rolling, padded table. I was taken from my mother's arms and placed on top of the stretcher table. As soon I was secured to the table, the medical team began running me through the halls toward the operating room. Even while running, the staff was double checking the attachments and making certain everything was in place. There was no time to spare. In order for me to survive, all of the medical staff knew that they had to act quickly.

    We burst through the double doors of the operating room. Each individual started working in different areas. They began cutting off the burnt clothes that were melted to my body. The staff began administering injections and inserting IVs. After this, the doctors placed a plastic covering of some kind over my mouth and nose area. After a few minutes, someone turned on a bright light overhead. I remember lying there and watching them all watching me, just waiting. I did not realize it at the time, but they were waiting for me to sleep so that they could do whatever was in their power to help me.

    I survived. I woke up in a hospital room a few days after that first surgery. I found out later that the head surgeon, after finishing the initial surgery, would not take me as a patient. He turned me over to his associate. Both men were fine physicians, but the doctor who initially worked on me had very personal reasons for not taking me as a patient. He felt he could not handle the emotional struggle that came with working with me as a patient. One year earlier, his own son at five years of age had been burned over 20% of his body and had died. The doctor said that every time he saw me, his mind would flash to memories of his own son, and he could not handle his emotions well enough to be my doctor.

When I first woke up two days later, my mind would fade in and out of consciousness. My memories of that first hospital stay are at best blurred and sketchy. I was in a bed, something like a large steel crib. I vaguely remember being strapped down to my bed in order to keep me from pulling out my IVs or doing something that could hinder my recovery. Over the bed, there was plastic-like material enclosing the crib like a tent. I assume that this tent was to protect against outside infections. Outside of my crib, there were machines everywhere.

I was in an excruciating pain. To my knowledge, in 1960, there were no burn centers, and the percentage of the population that had been through a major burn and survived was very slim. Due to this, I learned as I grew up that people seemed to have a hard time understanding what I had been through unless they had had a major burn themselves. Therefore, it is very hard for me to explain the level of pain I was feeling after that first surgery. It would be years later as a young man researching my injury that I would read that a major burn over 25% or more of the body was the most painful of all injuries. I still have no problem agreeing with this opinion.

    The hospital staff steadily monitored my progress. They kept me on a continual regimen of not only antibiotics but also pain medication. I am almost certain that the shots of pain medicine were morphine. I distinctly remember begging for more pain medicine, because the pain was so excruciating. There was no reprieve to my suffering. It seemed every breath I took in brought with it pain. The nurses would sympathetically inform me that they were giving me the maximum amount allowed. At six years of age, I did not understand what too much morphine could do to me. I only knew that I was still in a lot of pain.

At one point during this trying time, I began contemplating how I could stop the pain. It was overwhelming for me as a child.

My hospital room was on the third floor, and I had a window in my room. I was looking out my window one day when my mind lighted on an idea to end my pain. I began to consider the option of jumping. I was a relatively small boy, and this along with the burn had caused my body to weaken and become frail. I was also strapped to my bed. I knew that if I was going to jump, I needed someone to help me. Someone would have to release me from the bed and would also have to help me open the window. Accomplishing this on my own was not possible. As I lay there thinking it over, I finally worked up the courage to ask my mother to help me jump. As I talked with her, she began to cry. This image of my mother weeping has forever been with me; because as a child, I could not understand why she would cry. I was the one who was in pain. Years later, the tears that my mother shed on that day were finally understood.

My first hospital stay lasted about 5 weeks. I do not remember much about that period of time. Even as I try to recall now, the memories are fuzzy with only certain details that emerge in my memory. I remember not liking the food. Bologna sandwiches and oatmeal from home sounded much better to me. Later, it was shared with me that I screamed at the nurses to leave me alone. This has made me really appreciate what nurses have to put up with every day.

Finally, with the pain starting to subside and getting into a regular routine of bandage changes, I was able to go home. When I left the hospital, I looked like a mummy. The burn was from the waist up, chest and back, both arms, neck, and part of my face. These areas were bandaged to protect from infection. Not only were my burns bandaged, but my legs were bandaged as well. This was because they needed a lot of skin for the grafting process. They used most of the skin from my legs, both thighs and calves. The majority of my body was covered in bandages because of the burns and the damage from the grafting process. As a child, I had never been to the pyramids, or seen a mummy, but I believed I knew what a mummy must have felt like.

At home, my parents helped change the bandages regularly. Part of the bandaging process was burning the "proud" flesh from my skin. This was caused when the skin would grow slower than the flesh in the area of my wounds. If left to itself, the flesh would stick out through the skin around my wounds and keep the skin from healing together correctly. The doctor had to show my parents how to "burn" the proud flesh off my body. They used a silver nitrate stick to these protruding areas of flesh in order for my skin to heal in the best way possible.

    My parents also helped me with stretching exercises, which I would later learn was to help my contractures. The skin where the trauma occurred was burned and sealed, so it did not have elasticity. It did not grow and expand as normal skin did. The contractures affected the movement of muscle and the movement of skin. Without these stretching exercises, my body would have suffered more damage, because the skin from the burns would stick together. I had to stretch constantly in order for my skin to adjust to the contractures, as I still do to some extent.

    When the horrible itching began, it was as if my whole body itched at once, but because of all the bandages, I could not scratch the itch. (I wasn't supposed to anyway.) The itching was unbearable. I remember my mother finding some type of weight and using it to apply pressure to the bandage and then releasing it. While this was not scratching, it did seem to help. I knew I wasn't supposed to, but I found if I could get hold of some of the gauze in the inside of the bandage and slowly pull out a small piece from time to time, that would also relieve the itching. I wasn't very good at hiding the pieces I pulled out and would get fussed at for it.

My 6-year-old mind did not realize at the time that this burn would affect me for years to come. I would have to have many corrective surgeries and even plastic surgery. These surgeries were always scheduled during summer break from school. For many years the pattern was that I would have the surgery in the summer and go back to school with bandages and braces in the fall.

Some of the medical procedures seemed experimental. At times there were medical personnel, whole groups of them, looking at my burns and discussing the pros and cons of different opinions while standing around me. Once a doctor I didn't care for was claiming responsibility for some of the more successful surgeries. I spoke up and corrected him in front of the medical group, pointing to the less desirable results and making sure everyone knew he had done the "bad" surgeries. I remember naming the doctor who had done the good surgeries.

    I also had to wear corrective braces at times. These braces were worn around my neck, and they were hot and uncomfortable. They were used to try to expand the contractures of my burns. Before the accident, I was able to play and keep up with the children my age. After the accident, this was a totally different story. I was no longer able to run and play like I wanted. The things I wanted to enjoy, riding my bicycle, playing softball, all those childhood things had to be put off. Occasionally, I would get "special" help in order to be involved. This was especially hard for me, because I did not want to be looked at as different.

    If all the trauma to my body were not enough, I was severely affected by my emotions. You might think that since so many nerve endings were damaged from the burns that the damage would cause me to be emotional. While I'm sure that the nerve damage has affected my life, it is not the area which seemed to be my next experience.

After the accident, we moved to another house because of bad memories and financial difficulties. This house had no running water. The only heat was the fireplace and a wood stove. There was no air conditioner. We made do with box fans. In my heart, I felt that we moved from our home just because of me. I understood very early the financial problems my burns caused the family. I would overhear my parents discussing our money troubles, but they did not know I was listening. I struggled with guilt over causing my family to suffer. Late at night, I would lie in my bed in this rustic house, with no real heat and no air conditioning, and listen as my parents discussed our money troubles. They did not know how much I struggled.

After coming home from the hospital the first time and getting my bandages changed on a regular schedule two or three times a week, I was cleared by the doctors to go back to school in April of the same school year. I was so excited. I had made a lot of friends when I had started the first grade earlier that year, and I was excited to go back and see them. While in the hospital, so many people were so caring and supportive that I just knew all my friends in my class would be as well. On the morning of my first day of school, I was so excited. I was filled with anticipation. I thought that I would finally be able to go back to feeling like a normal kid again. I was wrong.

I remember walking into the school, so excited, but I did not receive the reaction that I thought I would get. There was no sympathy, no caring looks from the other students. No one reached out to tell me how glad they were that I was back. There were some children who, in retrospect, might have shown me kindness, but they were intimidated into silence by the other children. They were not able to stand up against the current. Looking back now, I guess the sight of the "mummy" and the medical odor that I exuded was overwhelming to them, because instead of the children receiving me and speaking nice to me, to my horror and humiliation, they made fun of me and mocked me cruelly. I was completely caught off guard. It was just such an abrupt change from how others had treated me in the hospital.

They held their noses because of the smell and nicknamed me "scar face" among other pet names. I became a sport to them. They were not content to leave me alone, but they hunted me down in order to amuse themselves. It got so bad that at recess I would run as fast as I could and try to find a bush or something on the playground to hide behind so that they couldn't make fun of me, but they hunted for me until they found where I was hiding. The children I once knew as friends would form a circle around me so I could not escape. They laughed at me and mocked me. They called me "scar face," "charcoal baby," and any other names they could think of associated with my burns and handicapped condition.

While some of the teachers tried to stop them from ridiculing me, I also remember some of the teachers, standing on the playground, watching, making no attempt to stop the children from their tormenting game. They seemed to turn a blind eye to what was going on right in front of them.

There were always some children who seemed to feel that it was their "mission" to scorn me. Some of the children were from the elite of our county, so this helped me understand very young that "elite" people had problems too.

Their penchant for torment seemed to have no end, so after awhile, I reached a point where I just gave up emotionally. I finally gave up hiding. I just accepted the mocking. I was like a beat down animal just accepting whatever was going to happen to me. I was traumatized emotionally. I dreaded going to school every day and facing the bullies that had made my life so miserable. Those were not very pleasant times. I do not have many good memories of school in those years. I tried to mentally block out all the hurt I could. My feelings seemed numb or dull. I tried not to complain too much at home, because I didn't want to be a cripple. I didn't want to be a burden. I wanted to run and play and do things like all the other kids. I just couldn't. I was only 6 years old, but I suppose this would not be easy to accept at any age. Those early days turned into months and years, and I spent those years taking abuse and suffering at the hands of those that were stronger than me. Finally, I reached a breaking point when I was in the fourth grade.

    I felt anger welling up on the inside. I decided that I had been beaten down and scorned long enough. I began to feel the urge to fight back against the cruelty that had been leveled against me. I knew it was time to stand up against them, but I wondered how. How do you fight back when you have handicaps like mine? I was a small boy to start with, and my body had become even weaker from the medical procedures. Even when I didn't have braces, I still had to contend with the burn contractures. I knew I could not move as fast or as well as the other kids my age. I began to wonder if I had any abilities or strengths to use besides those that were physical in nature.

With time, I began to realize that my "mind" seemed to work pretty well. I was able to learn quickly and grasp concepts well. I discovered a strength that I could use to my benefit. I began studying extra hard in school, but I did not always study for the right reasons. I did not always study for the joy of learning. My motive was to excel, so that I could embarrass the other children that did not have the same level of academic abilities as I had. I would make fun when they did not know the answer. If I could catch one putting down the wrong answer on the blackboard, I would call attention to their mistake in front of the whole classroom. This was good!

I especially enjoyed humiliating my tormentors, that group of "elite" kids, because, in my new found method for revenge, I felt they deserved a worse level of retribution. I also began wanting the teacher to call me to the chalkboard, not because I desired to experience the success of learning for learning's sake, but because I was able to make fun of others easier from the front of the room. It was also fun to find any mistake my teacher made. I found myself struggling with those in authority, because I did not feel I had been treated justly by some of them. They did not stop the mocking, so I made examples of them as well, though, I had to use a different approach while mocking the teachers.

    I also had to figure out a way to help myself physically. One way was to threaten the boys that were good at sports if they didn't let me play. When it was time for organized games supervised by the teachers, if these boys were team captains, I let them know that I did not want to be the last one picked. If that happened, they could be sure I would no longer help them with their math. Even this began to wear thin. I strove to have more physical success. I did not want to feel strong just mentally. I wanted to feel strong physically as well. With time, I found that a baseball bat and a large history book could be used for things other than what they were intended.

    I began to fight physically and had success with what I called my equalizers. I discovered that some spots on the body could not stand up as well as others, and several fast blows to those weak areas with an equalizer seemed to even up the odds very fast. I didn't worry about "fair" fighting. I figured there was nothing fair about what had been done to me, so I was not bound to others self-interpreted rules of fairness.

I became driven, mean spirited, and cruel. If I could reduce someone that was mean to me to tears over their poor grades or academic failures or leave them lying begging on the playground from a beating, I felt good. I felt right. I was proving myself their superior.

This type of thinking became such a part of me that it no longer mattered if they had done anything wrong to me. I was so tired of being beat down, that I just began to systematically mock or beat anyone I felt I could.

I was filled with rage toward those around me, and there did not seem to be an end to the path I was taking. Yet, there were people who tried to help me, including one teacher who seemed to take extra interest in me. She was aware of what I had been through, and she perceived what I was going through then. She tried to be my protector, shielding me from the perceived pressures. There was also a 4-H representative who was very kind. He tried to push me forward in leadership, because he felt there might be potential in me. While I appreciated their kindness and efforts, it still did not do much to stifle the rage inside.

The turning point that totally stopped me in my tracks came on quite unexpectedly.

On that day, I remember I was being hateful to my younger sister. My words were so cruel that she yelled at me to get away and stay away from her. She told me that I was so mean she couldn't stand me. Coming from my sister the words seemed totally out of character. They stopped me cold. For several days, I dwelt mentally on what she had said. I could not shake this feeling of unease. Slowly, a sort of understanding began to fill my mind. I began to see the truth of my actions. It was true I had literally been through the fire in my devastating accident. It was true that some of my fellow students had been cruel and hateful to me. It was equally true that I despised these things. Even though all of this was in fact true, it was also true that I had become just as hateful, cruel, and mean spirited as those people I hated for being mean to me, if not more so.

I had become the very thing that I "hated!"

I knew in my heart that that was not the person that I wanted to be. I began to wonder if I could change myself. I knew in my heart that I should not feel good about inflicting pain on other people. The fact that, not only was I willing to be cruel, but that I also enjoyed the feeling that came with hurting others was not something that I was not willing to admit to most people.

I began to ask myself, "How am I going to change?"

I did not realize it at the time, but looking back now I believe that the Lord had taken an interest in me. Some think of God as only sweet, kind, and benevolent. Others think of God as hard and judgmental. Of course, some do not even believe in God. But for me, God has become a caring power who wishes to lift people up, instructing us in positive ways. While He may judge us, He also desires that all will want the good things he offers.

One of the ways that I feel is necessary for a person to change is to see themselves for what they really are. Alcoholics, drug abusers, impulsive buyers, or whoever else, all have to understand that they have a problem before they can change.

This was an experience that, while it was painful at the time, I am so grateful it happened to me.

The Lord stripped back any self justification and let me see my cruelty, mocking, and violent behavior for what it truly was. I was a horrible person on the inside. No matter how hard I tried to hide it from some, there was no way I could hide it from all. Suddenly, I felt nothing but shame and disgust with myself, with what I had let myself become.

In my family, there was a religious tone that was fairly stable and fairly mixed. It was stable in the sense that the Bible was promoted as the truth, and Jesus was held up as the only answer. It was mixed in the sense that my mother had been raised Lutheran and my father had been raised Pentecostal. The church we attended was a community church in that it was not affiliated with any one religious organization. Our ministers were whoever would come and preach to a small country church. I bring this up now, because you will see in time that this background helped shape my questions and helped shape the solutions to the situation in which I found myself. I began to realize that the one common area that all these individuals shared was that they all looked to the Bible as the answer.

Looking back now, I felt bad about my behavior and even worse about the feelings inside that I was hoping to hide from others. I wanted to "feel good" about my life, but I wasn't even sure what to feel good about!

I began asking questions. I was in a very precarious position, because I felt, by instinct I suppose, that a question could also indicate how I felt inside. At that point, I was still hoping to hide that part of my life the best I could. I asked my parents about the Bible and how to "get right" with the Lord. I was told to repent for anything that I had done wrong, and the Lord would forgive me. I repented like I was told, but I did not feel much peace. I continued to feel bad on the inside. Instead of finding peace and joy like I had hoped, I began remembering and seeing some of the faces of those that I had been cruel to and mocked and beat up.

I went to my mother and confided to her that I did not feel very successful with this repenting stuff, and she suggested it might help if I apologized to anyone that I had wronged. (If she only knew what this would entail!) Even the thought of apologizing to anyone of them seemed so hard. I kept trying to put it out of my mind, but it seemed like the Lord wanted me to "fix" some of these areas. Every time I would pray, these images of the cruelty that I had inflicted would come to my mind. The reason I say "some of these areas" is because I believed there was no way I could remember all the hateful things I had done. I did not feel it necessary to repent to those whom I had only had bad thoughts about. I mainly felt that I needed to repent to those that I had physically fought in childhood battle.

So, in obedience, I began repenting to different ones. While this was hard, I wanted something in return; I wanted to feel real inner peace. Most of the children that I repented to were simply caught off guard and told me that it was fine. They seemed to want to forget it as much as I did, but there was one situation that really tested my apologetic resolve.

One particular boy had really upset me when I had fought him, so I saved repenting to him for last. Finally the time came for me to repent to him. I summoned my courage and apologized, but instead of the forgiveness I had received from the other kids, his reaction was totally unexpected. He mocked me again! I was so infuriated, I beat him up again. When I prayed about it later, I felt I had to repent again. After several days, I approached the boy again to repent to him. He simply mocked me again. Once again, I became so angry that I beat him up. When I prayed later, I still felt the Lord wanted me to repent again but this time to repent successfully. After a period of time, I repented to the boy again, and he mocked me once again. This time I stood there, and I took his ridicule without beating him up again. I felt like every part of my body was on fire again. While I did not find the peace I was looking for, I was glad that I had kept myself under control at last, that is, at least that time.

    During all of this time, I continually prayed for the inner peace I desperately wanted. While I would seem to touch it briefly at times, I was still usually full of anger. I have heard people say that they experienced "righteous indignation," but this was not what I was feeling. I began to realize that not only did I have anger—I had a lot of it! I was angry over the pain of the burns. I was angry when I had to wear the braces. I was angry about my body being covered with scars. I was angry at the children who had mocked me. I was angry at the teachers who didn't seem to be able to stop them. I was angry at the hand life had dealt me. I was angry at the world, and I was angry at God.

    I became aware of just how much anger raged within me. As I struggled to deal with my flood of churning emotions, these feelings of anger seemed overwhelming. I was still a child, and I realize now that this was almost too much emotion for a little kid to have to carry. But now that I had finally acknowledged the depth and extent of this overwhelming anger, what could I do about it? Unfortunately, this created a new problem.

    While the anger issue was a major problem, it seemed like the dam broke, and I was being flooded from all directions. One problem seemed to touch another problem, and that problem seemed to touch another area, and so on and so on. I found in trying to deal with anger I was also dealing with pride. I soon realized that some type of plan to deal with these things was needed. I must have been born with an innate ability to plan things. Later in life, I asked my mother how I behaved before the burn, and she told me that I had already exhibited an ability to plan and that I distanced myself from others when there was conflict. Certainly, this ability to plan helped me in the journey that I was about to take.

    I began to formulate a plan in my mind, but implementing this plan while a flood of emotion continually washed over me created a problem. It was kind of like trying to mow the yard in the middle of a rainstorm. While the yard might really need mowing, you just have to wait, to hold on until you can begin doing something about it. The rain will stop, and you can begin to mow. With patience, the yard will get mowed.

    In looking back, I don't think that I ever verbally expressed my plan on what to do with where I was. I just made a concrete decision on what to do with all my problems. I decided that I would go to the Bible for all my solutions! This may sound simple, but that was it. There had been a lot of searching for the answers that I needed. As I share with you the path that I started on so many years ago, I will let you make a decision about whether or not my choices created a successful outcome.

    While anger and pride were to be a part of the journey, learning to look to the Bible for direction, for setting a goal that would be sustaining over and over again would be the bigger part. Let me now share with you, step-by-step, my journey.

Chapter 2

How Do I Get Rid Of Anger?

This was a perplexing problem. How does one rid themselves of such a strong emotion that has such deep roots in the heart. I had spent years feeding my anger and allowing these emotions to have so much room in my life. Many whims that my anger desired, I had succumbed to. Many opportunities had been presented to feed this desire, and I usually gave in and did whatever felt good. But once I knew I needed to change, I felt like I was running backwards in a crowd full of people moving forward.

Needing answers and finding none, I had decided to go to the Bible and God for those answers. It felt awkward when I first started this journey because, at this point, I was still angry at God. It felt strange to pray to God for help with my anger while at the same time being angry at Him for what had happened to me. It was hard to feel so much anger toward Him and, by the same token, ask Him for help. Even so, I had been told all my life that only God held the answers, so I decided this was the logical place to start the journey. Slowly, I put my emotions of anger towards God to the side and began to seek His assistance. I knew I could not change my nature on my own—I had to have his help. Even at that early age, I was able to understand that one slip at the wrong time could cause me to get into serious trouble. I knew if I did not get my anger under control I could very easily do something unlawful, something that I could not take back. The path I had been on was going to lead me to a juvenile facility or even possibly to prison. One of my friends had already gotten into trouble, and it landed him in reform school. Even at my young age, I had firsthand knowledge of friends and acquaintances who had made mistakes, mistakes that cost them a steep price. I had seen the results of following that path, and I knew that was not where my answers were.

I began working very hard to control my outward demonstrations of anger. This somewhat concealed my anger from others, but it was still there, churning inside me.

I am reminded of a story told to me about a little boy named Johnny. Johnny was in class, and the teacher told him to sit down. Little Johnny did not want to sit down. This teacher had to tell him several times to sit down. Finally, he did obey the teacher, but he told his teacher that even though he had sat down, he was still standing on the inside. The moral of this story is that even though one outwardly displays a particular trait, this may run incredibly contrary to what is on the inside. This is the point I was at in my life. I was trying to behave on the outside, but I could still feel rage on the inside. While this facade may be deemed acceptable in polite society, it was not how I wanted to feel on the inside. I felt like I had an animal in a cage on the inside. I did not want to feel this way forever. I wanted peace. I began to ask God to help me. I was still was not certain this would help, but I figured the only way I would know for sure if God's solution would work was to try it.

I know this all sounds rather elementary, but is it really? What do you do if you are putting together a cabinet, and you find a piece that you do not recognize? Logic asserts that you go to the manual and read the instructions. That is simply what I was attempting to do. I knew I wanted help from the Lord, so I went to the instruction manual to find it. I went to the Bible. This meant that I had to read the manual to learn what the instructions said. I began to read the Bible.

It would have been very easy if there would have been a specific section that was labeled "Anger," but I found this was not so. I found when reading and studying my Bible that it seemed to jump from one section to another rather quickly. I would look up the word "anger" in my concordance, and the next verse seemed to be on a completely different subject. As a novice when it came to studying the Bible, I did find this very challenging.

I did not realize it at first, but the journey I had embarked on would prove to be a rather long one. Life's problems would not be solved in a day, certainly not like in a sitcom. The situations that we deal with are not always, in fact most likely *never*, wrapped in a nice, neat package and resolved in a 30-minute timeslot. So I began my journey with baby steps, in particular, with these two passages:

"Dearly beloved, avenge not yourselves, but rather give place unto wrath: for it is written, Vengeance is mine; I will repay, saith the Lord." (Rom. 12:19)

"But I say unto you, That ye resist not evil: but whosoever shall smite thee on thy right cheek, turn to him the other also." (Matt. 5:39)

I did not particularly like these passages in the Bible. They made me upset. I just wanted to shut my Bible and quit, because I did not like the instructions I was getting. Even though I was upset, I knew I could not give up so easily. I began to think on these passages. They made me angry, because they made me appear weak. They also seemed to let those wrongdoers go free.

I went to my father with my concerns. I expressed to him that walking away from a fight seemed weak to me. My father's response was a simple one. He said that it took a stronger man to walk away from a fight than to stick around just to show that he could win. This really did not make any sense to me. Throughout all my experiences, I personally found that I felt better when I fought and won than when I walked away. It seemed to me that running away meant that I was admitting that I was unable to beat my opponent. I would have rather taken a beating than to admit up front I could not win. I suppose this was pride on my part, but I would rather have the knowledge that I had tried and lost than not to have tried at all. Giving in to the fight brought the better feeling of satisfaction, but I could definitely understand how it was harder to walk away. It certainly was for me.

On a positive note, this quality if converted can be an admirable characteristic. There are things in this life that are worth fighting for. I just needed to learn to focus this trait in the right direction. At this time, I was fighting for the wrong things. I was fighting for things that, in the end, would destroy me if I did not get them under control. Although I did not like or particularly enjoy the idea of turning the other cheek, I knew I needed to try. To get the results I wanted, I knew I had to put my whole heart into it. Even in my youth, I knew that a half hearted effort would garner an incomplete result. I do have to admit, however, that even while giving it my best, I still failed at times. I kept trying, though. Proverbs says that "a just man falleth seven times, and riseth up again"[1] I fell many times, but I did not give up. I enjoyed the successes I had and learned from the failures. Taken correctly, even failure can bring good results.

     While implementing this act of walking away, I learned that people did not always understand. They did not realize that for me it was much harder to walk away. What they perceived as weakness was actually strength. I had to learn for myself that developing an inner control was not weak. I began to realize that proving you could win just for the sake of winning did not a strong person make. I also had to learn not to worry about what others perceived

---

[1] Proverbs 24:16

but only what I knew was right. This did not happen overnight. It was a slow, gradual process.

"For that which I do I allow not: for what I would, that do I not; but what I hate, that do I." (Rom. 7:15)

This scripture is a good example of what I felt on the inside. There was a war going on in there. I wanted to do what was right, but my nature would rise up and try to overpower what I knew the Bible said to do. This constant struggle in and of itself began to strengthen me. I began to notice that in my successes and failures, there was a huge difference between self discipline and strength through prayer seeking God continually. As stated earlier, I could keep the animal in the cage for a time, but there was still an animal. I wanted to get rid of the animal. I wanted to rid myself of the negative anger that had consumed me for so long. There was no way to do this through self discipline. At the same time, self discipline is not to be disregarded. I encourage everyone to use self discipline in order to be productive naturally. The more discipline we exercise in our day-to-day life, the more successful we can be naturally.

I found that the more I learned to lean on the Lord, the more strength I found. The benefits from truly trusting God and from prayer are without measure. I began to enjoy an inner calm that far surpassed the benefits of using self discipline alone.

"But I say unto you, That ye resist not evil: but whosoever shall smite thee on thy right cheek, turn to him the other also." (Matt. 5:39)

I also began to come to terms with the thought that this passage simply allowed the wrongdoers to get away with their wrongdoings. For example, Matthew 26:11 says, *"For ye have the poor always with you; but me ye have not always."* There will always be wrong in the world. Human nature in its unrestrained form has an inherently evil side. This passage shows that greed will always be around as long as there is human nature that is left unchecked. I Timothy 6:10 says, *"For the love of money is the root of all evil: which while some coveted after, they have erred from the faith, and pierced themselves through with many sorrows."* It is not money itself that is evil. It is the love of money that is evil. It is this love of money that feeds the greed that is so evident in the world around us.

At this moment, there seems to be enough food in the world to feed most of the hungry people on the face of earth, but this does not always happen because of the greed that prevails in our society. A foreign dictator once stated that it is easier to keep control over people when they are hungry than when they are fed. This is not an uncommon reasoning in the world.

Gradually, I began to understanding that wrongdoers were part of a bigger setting that I could not handle by myself. One of the reasons that God reserves certain types of judgment for himself alone is that we, in our human frailty, allow emotions to cloud our judgement. This is one of the reasons that a rule of law has a place in society. It is very difficult to make logical decisions when you are involved personally with the wrongdoing. It is hard to be objective in a situation when you are the one who was hurt. That is why it is best to allow God to handle the wrong that we see around us. God is able to judge logically and not based on human emotions. This helped me come to terms with letting what I perceived as wrongs go unpunished.

     I remember once as an adult having a person explain to me the way he was going to handle his involvement in the settling of an estate. He decided that he was going to block an inheritance procedure, because his great uncle had done him wrong. He was upset to the point that a deep bitterness had taken root in his heart. He decided that no one would benefit from the inheritance because of what had been done to him. It did not matter to him that the uncle was already dead and no one else had participated in the perceived wrongdoing. It was very hard for me to understand the position this man had taken due to the intense anger he was experiencing. He was willing to suffer himself in order to keep anyone else from benefiting from this inheritance. That man, along with everyone else involved, would have benefited so much more from trusting God's instructions.

As I began to study other individuals and their problems with anger, the bigger this little word "anger" seemed to grow. There are times when dealing with one's own anger that they will inevitably have to deal with the anger of others. I became much more aware of anger, and I saw anger in many different people. Anger was not limited to a certain age or station in life. Anger was evident in people all around me from the people sitting behind me in the church house to the kids that I played with on the playground. Anger was no respecter of persons. I believe that we all must come to the point that we see our anger and understand that it has to be acknowledged and dealt with on a daily basis. There will always be situations or triggers in our life that cause anger to rise in us. Some triggers will be small, like driving in heavy traffic, something we have all probably experienced. Some triggers will be much larger, such as someone hurting someone that we love. Triggers large and small have the potential to create anger. The thing that we have to understand is that controlling or extinguishing our anger will not be something that is dealt with or accomplished in a day. You will not wake up one morning and just have all of your anger disappear. You will have to deal with anger as it arises and understand that as humans, we will deal with these emotions the rest of our lives. It is a part of our nature. The important thing is that it is dealt with. Unresolved anger can lead to bitterness, and a bitter path does not lead to a life of peace and joy. It is quite the opposite.

     The next thing that I had to ask myself was if "turning the other cheek" was always the right option. I began to wonder if there was a clearcut, black-and-white answer to this question. Would all situations be handled the same or did the situations vary depending upon the circumstances? Where did one draw the boundary lines in every day life and still be pleasing in the sight of the Lord? What kind of anger was acceptable to experience in our hearts and still have peace when we laid our heads down at night? These were just some of the questions that this passage brought to my mind. I began to study the scriptures to find an answer. In my studies, I also found scriptures that seemed in my mind to be very different from the concept of turning the other cheek. I felt the Bible would not contradict itself, so I knew that there had to be an explanation.

One of the first scriptures that I noticed involved Jesus. In John 2:14-15, the Bible states, *"And found in the temple those that sold oxen and sheep and doves, and the changers of money sitting: And when he had made a scourge of small cords, he drove them all out of the temple, and the sheep, and the oxen; and poured out the changers' money, and overthrew the tables."* When I read this scripture, it did not seem to me that Jesus was turning the other cheek. In fact, he was angry enough that he made a whip of cords and drove the people out of the temple. Even as I picture this in my mind now, I am certain that it was not done in a sweet manner. He was angry at what was going on in the temple. The temple was a place of purity, and it so angered him to see it turned into a marketplace that his wrath resulted in the destruction by Christ of the market that they had set up. Reading this as a child, my first thought was that if Jesus could get this angry, then I should be able to do so as well. I had been told all my life by my elders that Jesus was perfect, so I knew that his anger could not be wrong.

Proverbs 25:23 was another affirming passage that I came across. It states, *"The north wind driveth away rain: so doth an angry countenance a backbiting tongue."* This passage implies that just as a north wind stops rain, an angry face could stop a backbiting tongue. It seems to give permission to have a harsh or angry face when we are approached by a backbiting or backstabbing individual. Showing an angry face may cause this person to check what they are saying before they say it. Anger seems to be used as a stone-walling tool in this passage.

The Apostle Paul writes in Ephesians 4:26, *"Be ye angry, and sin not: let not the sun go down upon your wrath:"* This passage really made me begin to question the subject of anger. Could it be possible that I could feel anger and not be evil? Is some anger neither sinful nor displeasing to God? All my life I have heard people around me loosely use the term "righteous indignation."

While this concept is correct and there are times when anger is acceptable, we must be very careful about declaring a person or situation "righteous." This concept is not one to be used lightly. The danger in justifying every angry outburst as righteous indignation is that it can cause us to begin to justify even the wrong choices that we make. The more that we justify a situation, the less we feel that we have done anything wrong. If I do nothing wrong, then where does that put me? This is a very precarious outlook. We must be very careful that we do not try to use these scriptures to justify anger that is, in fact, not at all righteous in God's eyes.

Matthew 5:40 is another passage that seems to be in this same vein. It states, *"**And if any man will sue thee at the law**, and take away thy coat, let him have thy cloak also..."* If someone had the opportunity to sue me, then this implies that I did not turn the other cheek too quickly. What if the verdict had been in my favor, would the instructions have been the same? Would I still be instructed to let this individual have my cloak also if the law found that I was in the right?

With all of the different scriptures that I was studying during this time in my life, I could not find any absolute answer that would apply to every situation. There was no black and white solution to every problem that would come up. There will always be "gray" in our day-to-day situations. With all of these passages, there did not seem to be a rule that stated that turning the other cheek meant that we should just lay down and play dead anytime something came up. It takes time and wisdom to understand where the lines are supposed to be drawn. This is what I began to question in my own life. I desperately wanted to know where I was supposed to draw the lines in dealing with my own anger. I knew that my end goal was peace with God and peace within myself. This is what I wanted. Finally, in my own personal journey, I settled on two areas that I would focus my energy and time dealing with.

The Biblical answer to the first area I chose to deal with was found in a passage in Paul's letter to the church at Ephesus, or Ephesians. Paul writes in chapter four and verse twenty-six that we are not to let the sun go down on our wrath. Not only do I try to not sin when anger comes, I try to not "hold" it for very long. As I stated previously, I have found that holding anger creates bitterness. This bitterness is a lot harder to deal with than anger in its early stages. It is like having a tree in a garden. If you pull on the young tree in its early stages, it is rather easy to pull it out, roots and all. The longer that the tree is left to itself, the deeper the roots will go down into the garden. It is no longer "easy" to pull out. It is not impossible to get rid of, but it takes a lot more effort. Instead of gently pulling it out, you would need tractors, backhoes, saws, and a lot more manpower. This is the same with bitterness, once it is allowed to germinate in our heart, its roots run deep in our hearts, and it takes a great deal of effort to rid ourselves of it. It will be to our own benefit to deal with anger as it comes instead of letting it fester day-in and day-out in our hearts.

    I also began to question in my heart what was so wrong with being angry at someone that had hurt an innocent person. I finally came to the conclusion that this anger is not necessarily wrong. God uses this anger and allows it in us in its proper place to help motivate us to do the things that we should.

There will be times in trying to amend our angry way of living that people will not understand. There will be some that want you to be angry and some that think you have no right to be angry. There will always be someone who thinks that you are not doing right, regardless of how you act.

I am reminded of a story once told to me. It involves a boy, a father, and their mule. The boy and his father had made a trip into town to buy their mule. On the journey home, the boy and his father walked past a group of people and heard them remark how ridiculous it was that nobody was riding the mule. The father then decided to let his son ride the mule to keep from offending if anyone else came along. It was not long before they did encounter another person. This time they heard the person mumbling that it was so terrible that the son had so little respect for the elderly. Upon hearing this, the father then took his son off the mule and rode it himself. Surely this would appease the next passerby. After a short time, they passed another person on the way home. This time, the person remarked that it was child abuse to make the son lead the mule while the father rode the mule. The father and son were flabbergasted by this. Finally, they thought they had the perfect solution. They would both ride the mule. After riding along for a few miles, they encountered yet another person on their journey. This time, the person was disgusted to see such a blatant display of animal abuse. The father and son got off the mule and decided that the only option would be to carry the mule. So they tied its legs, ran a pole through the rope, and carried the mule on their shoulders. The next person they passed remarked that it was insane to be carrying a perfectly good mule that could walk. The moral of this story is that there is no way to please everybody. In dealing with anger or any problem that you may be dealing with, the most important concern is to *please God*.

     The next thing in my journey that I began to deal with was found in Matthew 6:11-12. This passages states, *"Give us this day our daily bread. And forgive us our debts, **as** we forgive our debtors."* Of course, this is a very recognizable part of the Lord's Prayer. The part I want to focus on is the tiny little word **as**. There are times in my life that I have made mistakes and slipped. My hope is that as time goes on, I will gradually begin to slip less and less. This passages indicates that the Lord ties any successes that we have to how we treat others. He will only forgive us if we forgive others. The Lord is very clear that he wants us to treat others in the same way that we would want to be treated. Another place this is seen is in Matthew 5:7. This passage says, *"Blessed are the merciful: for they shall obtain mercy."* He will show us mercy if we show others mercy. This concept is seen throughout the Bible. I do not want to get angry with people every time I perceive that they are not treating me right. After all these years, I know that human nature is flawed. I will struggle no matter how "good" I am in my efforts to restrain myself. I know that I need mercy and forgiveness in my life on a daily basis, so there are times when people are mistreating me that I will silently begin to pray for God to forgive them and have mercy on their shortcomings. You might think that this in itself makes me "good." In reality, I sometimes feel a little selfish. The reason for this is that I know that I need mercy, so I know I must show mercy. It is a lot easier to be merciful to others when you realize your own need for mercy.

The passage in Matthew 6 also mentions the phrase, "...*give us this day our **daily** bread...*" This implies that this prayer is a daily prayer. It also shows that the Lord wants us to handle things on a daily basis. I ask myself daily if there is anything that I need to fix. I have found personally in my own life that it has a positive impact if I check myself every day and try to handle anger if I find any. This daily process is how I have learned to handle my anger and how I have found peace on the inside.

As stated earlier, this process may not be the same for every person. This is simply the path I took to help me deal with the issues that I had in my life. I would soon find, however, that in dealing with my anger, there would be other emotions that would rise up that were just as challenging to deal with.

Chapter 3

Pride

As I tried to solve the problem of anger in my life, I ran into other issues. I found that anger was intertwined with many other feelings. In fact, it seemed that every situation I decided to work on was intertwined with many other areas in my life. Therefore, I would have to "multitask" (to use a current day buzzword) when dealing with my emotions. I found as I struggled to change my pattern and deal with the anger in my heart, pride turned out to be a pretty big issue as well.

Throughout my years of study, I have found that there are varying opinions on problems with human emotions. With every opinion often comes another supposed solution. As a boy, it was easiest for me if I just dealt with things as they came along. Of course, every person is different. This is simply what worked best for me. I am not trying to say that my solution is the only answer. In fact, some may view my solution as too different, difficult, or even too simple. I really do not feel this is the case. If a solution works, then how can it be wrong? The point is that, in using my solution, from my perspective, I was able to come closer to reaching my goal, which was to have peace with God and to be pleasing in His eyes. I do not have any doubts that there are many different ways that people deal with their own issues. This was my journey, so I walked it the best way that I knew how. As in life, much of the time, there is usually more than one path to reach a certain destination!

I discovered pride in my life fairly early. My first instances of recognizing self-pride were when it came to apologizing to others. At times, it was the only thing that would keep me from repenting, especially when I knew that I was in the wrong. I believe we have all felt this at times. It is that feeling that rises up when we know we are wrong, but we just do not want to admit it. This is pride, and I had it in abundance.

I came to learn as I began to grow in my walk with the Lord, that pride could blind me when it came to making decisions.

The sin of pride is not altogether an unpleasant emotion. At times, I felt good even when I was clearly wrong. I heard it said once that it was a shame that pride was a sin, because it felt so good. There is a lot of truth in the emotional part of this saying. It creates an emotion in us that is not entirely logical. Pride, rearing its unbiblical head, can be a very strange creature.

One might think that pride is not really that much of an issue, but it can be very detrimental to us in our daily walk. Pride can be counterproductive in many ways. It oftentimes gets in the way of us accepting things that we need. If we let our pride get in the way consistently, it can hinder us from hearing instructions and accepting needed guidance. At times the unwillingness to admit that help is needed or that you might be wrong is rooted in pride. This can lead to us having problems that, in true humble spirit, are completely avoidable. It is not always easy, but it is necessary to put aside pride in order to be successful not just spiritually but naturally as well.

I began to study this subject, as well, and found the following scriptures that made an impression on me as a young man.

"The wicked in his pride doth persecute the poor: let them be taken in the devices that they have imagined. For the wicked boasteth of his heart's desire, and blesseth the covetous, whom *the LORD abhorreth. The wicked, through the pride of his countenance, will not seek after God: God is not in all his thoughts." (Psalm 10:2-4)*

This scripture shows that pride can and will get in the way of our relationship with God. I have heard many times people say that they had control of their own life, and their life was pretty good. To think that one does not need God is prideful. The Bible says that it is wicked to feel this way.

"The fear of the LORD is to hate evil: pride, and arrogancy, and the evil way, and the froward mouth, do I hate." (Proverbs 8:13)

From reading this scripture, it seems that part of our responsibility in fearing the Lord is to hate pride. God does not command this without reason. He knows what pride can lead to if left unchecked in our lives. It leads us away from

Him. God wants to draw us closer. Therefore, we need to get rid of anything in our life that would hinder our walk with Him.

"Only by pride cometh contention: but with the well advised is wisdom." (Proverbs 13:10)

Contention in this scripture means the act of striving in controversy. The feeling of wanting to be right and having the last word is based in pride. When we have pride in our life, it causes us to have contention with those around us.

"The pride of thine heart hath deceived thee, thou that dwellest in the clefts of the rock, whose habitation is high; that saith in his heart, Who shall bring me down to the ground?" (Obadiah 1:3)

I finally realized in order to deal with my anger I also had to deal with my pride. It was a struggle for me to say that I was sorry for the things that I had done in anger. For me, this was an admission that I was wrong. Viewing this through my prideful eyes, the act of admitting I was wrong was an embarrassment in itself. The part that was embarrassing was that I had to publicly acknowledge that I had been cruel, mean, and despicable. It is hard to admit that you are wrong even when you know that it is true and clear to everyone around you. I began to realize that as humiliating as this was, I still needed to repent. Some say that apologizing is a sign of weakness, but sometimes your wrongdoing is so obvious by almost everyone that even the act of refusing to admit you are wrong makes you look small. I knew this was where I was. Everyone could already see how badly I had behaved regardless of whether or not I repented. It was pride that was keeping me from repenting and making things right with those I had wronged.

I came to the realization that anger makes us do terrible things, and pride helps to promote the wrongs even further by leaving them in place.

There is a passage in the Bible that states ***"Confess your faults one to another****, and pray one for another, that ye may be healed. The effectual fervent prayer of a righteous man availeth much." (James 5:16)*

This scripture passage reads kind of easy until you try to practice this instruction. Just as I had to admit I had a problem with anger in order to start getting help, I also had to admit that I had a problem with pride to make progress in the goal that I had set in my life. I did not want pride to get in the way of having the internal peace that I so longed for in my life. Although the anger was easier to spot in my life, pride could be deadlier because it was more subtle.

A popular mantra in our society today is that we must believe in ourselves in order to succeed. This idea of self confidence is promoted heavily all around us. Even from childhood, we are taught that if we just believe in ourselves, we can do anything. I know that many will say that this is true, but for me I found that I had to be careful with believing in myself too much. By believing in myself too much, I could justify my feelings and position easier. Justifying one's position might have some merit if you are always right. This will never be the case. We will all be wrong at some point in our lives. When pride was plentiful in my mind, I found that it was easier to justify myself even when ultimately I came to understand I was wrong all along.

    Correcting and identifying pride in my life became needful for me, because when left unchecked, my understanding of a situation was blurred. Instead of working towards good solutions, pride caused me to blame others for all of the problems in my life. While it was true that others had wronged me, as long as I focused on their faults, I did not look at my own faults. I realized that to have inward peace I would be required to look inward. I would never reach this goal in my own heart if I focused on everyone else's problems instead of my own. Looking outward would never bring about the solution to my problem. I had to work out my own salvation. Peace would only come by changing my own heart. Pride gets in the way of this. If we can't admit that it is our own faults that keep us in turmoil, we will never have the peace that God is holding out to us.

Pride was a monumental struggle in my life. I was too proud to repent. I was too proud to admit I might be at fault. I was too proud to accept instruction I didn't like.

I had used pride like a wall to block out all the hurt and pain surrounding me. When I look back, I don't remember for sure what I was so proud about in my life.

This issue is one that almost everyone struggles with. When you think about it, who likes their faults pointed out? Proverbs 18:17 states, *"He that is first in his own cause seemeth just: but his neighbor cometh and searcheth him."* Even though it does not feel good at the time, it is sometimes necessary for people around us to show us where we are wrong. In my own life, I have found benefit to listening to people criticize me and even saying hateful things to me. Even though the person being critical may have had the wrong attitude, I tried not to let my pride and anger automatically cast their words aside. I would try to listen and later meditate on the words and ask myself, "What if they were right?"

      This was good for me, because I had come to a rocky place on my path. I found it hard to accept instruction even from the Bible. There were always people around willing to give me advice, but I had come to the place that I could easily brush aside most advice based on one thought, the thought that "You have not been through what I've been through, so what do you know about my problems?" I had made it a practice to brush aside the advice from people that I felt had no idea what I was dealing with, but for me to brush aside the Bible was something different. Even though I was angry at God at times, I tried to be careful about casting aside His instruction. Even though it was not always easy to overcome my pride, I gradually learned to receive.

*"Therefore **pride compasseth them about as a chain**; violence covereth them as a garment.." (Psalm 73:6)*

    I began to realize that pride was a chain that could hold me bound and stop me from doing the things that I should do. I found that pride consistently hindered me from being able to receive instructions properly. I struggled with the ability to accept instruction in my life. Therefore, I found myself at times "changing" the advice so that I was always "comfortable."

    After I came home from the hospital with my burns for the first time, the doctors had given my parents instructions on how to change my bandages so that I wouldn't have to go back as often. One of the areas that needed attention in the process was my proud flesh and what I could do about it. Proud flesh was a term used to describe a condition where the flesh would stick up past the first layer of skin and keep the wound edges from being able to come together and heal properly.

 The solution to this problem was to use a nitrate stick. These nitrate sticks were used as cauterizing agents. Using the nitrate, we had to touch the proud flesh until it burned down to the level of the skin. This procedure had an awful smell. It smelled like burning flesh. That is exactly what it was, flesh being burnt off me.

 There were times in my life that I could compare the burning of proud flesh to my pride. Sometimes, the pride would have to be "burnt" out. It was not a pleasant prospect at times. It was painful, but it was needed for proper healing to occur. My attitude needed to "heal," and pride was getting in the way. I came to understand that the right way would not always be the easy way.

*"The **wicked, through the pride of his countenance, will not seek after God**: God is not in all his thoughts." (Psalm 10:4)*

I wanted to learn to live in a frame of mind where I was willing to receive proper instruction. While there were always plenty of opinions around, they would not always agree. Plus, I didn't want just any answer, I wanted the right solution. However simplistic this may sound, I would learn to lean more and more on the Bible as the final authority.

"Blessed are the poor in spirit, for theirs is the kingdom of Heaven." *(Matt. 5:3)*

When I think of this scripture, I think of a glass of water. If you have a glass that is already full of water, then you will not be able to get any more water in the glass, no matter what you try. The concept of not being able to put more water in an already full glass was an image that I could understand. As long as I was full of myself, the concepts of the Bible would have a hard time finding their way in. We must be willing to empty ourselves of our own spirit, which pride is a part of, to be able to have more of His Spirit in our lives.

    To empty out my pride on a regular basis has been an ongoing struggle. My goal has been to empty out my own opinions, justification of my positions, and "self" from my mind and replace them with instructions from the Bible. This goal was difficult when I started working on it, and it has remained challenging even until now. This effort has become a daily activity, like pulling weeds along a garden pathway. If you let the weeds grow too long, it is very difficult to rid them from the garden. Whenever I became aware of pride springing up, I tried to pluck it immediately to keep it from taking too deep a root in my life. The longer pride is left alone, the harder it is to get control over.

While I have come to the place that I work on pride willingly, I have also found that conditions in our lives can literally force us to work on our pride. For me personally, my scars, limited physical ability, and people staring at me because of the results of my injuries has made me deal with my pride. I had to come to the place that I could in some way try to use these experiences in a "positive" way. If I did not, then bitterness could creep in and these experiences could consume me in a negative way. I did not want this in my life.

One of the passages that had a major impact on my life is found in Luke 17:1-10. This passage states, *"Then said he unto the disciples, It is impossible but that offences will come: but woe unto him, through whom they come! It were better for him that a millstone were hanged about his neck, and he cast into the sea, than that he should offend one of these little ones. Take heed to yourselves: If thy brother trespass against thee, rebuke him; and if he repent, forgive him. And if he trespass against thee seven times in a day, and seven times in a day turn again to thee, saying, I repent; thou shalt forgive him. And the apostles said unto the Lord, Increase our faith. And the*

Lord said, If ye had faith as a grain of mustard seed, ye might say unto this sycamine tree, Be thou plucked up by the root, and be thou planted in the sea; and it should obey you. But which of you, having a servant plowing or feeding cattle, will say unto him by and by, when he is come from the field, Go and sit down to meat? And will not rather say unto him, Make ready wherewith I may sup, and gird thyself, and serve me, till I have eaten and drunken; and afterward thou shalt eat and drink? Doth he thank that servant because he did the things that were commanded him? I trow not. So likewise ye, when ye shall have done all those things which are commanded you, say, We are unprofitable servants: we have done that which was our duty to do."

    As I was studying on faith one day, I began to consider that this passage on duty was an instruction in faith building. The part that touched my pride the most, like the nitrate stick touching my proud flesh, was the fact that there seemed to be so "little" appreciation for all the effort. I, as most people would, like to feel appreciated, accepted, and praised. This unprofitable servant idea for me was a pride "buster." I believe that if you try this honestly and properly, you will find it helps drive pride out.

I'd like to step back for a moment and say that I realize that there are many views on how to "fix" our lives. I don't want to come across to you like my experiences or views are the only way, but this is how things have worked for me. Sometimes, I hear people sharing their experiences, and they sound so different from mine. For instance, some have said that they were "saved" or received something from God "instantly." They would then use that thought to imply that "everything" was all right between them and God on a permanent basis. This is completely different than what I have experienced in my life. My experiences, while having decision-making turns all along the way, have been more like a journey. I would identify a problem and then work on that problem until I found some success, which would in turn bring more internal peace.

Chapter 4

Establishing Guides in Using the Bible

As I read and studied the Bible for answers, I began to realize that I needed some way to set guides or methods to study by. There were many reasons I felt this was needed. The Bible is vast and can be overwhelming at first if not studied in an organized way.

Let me give you a few examples.

One: When I asked advice from different individuals, they had opinions of what the Bible would mean, but the opinions would change from one individual to another individual. Therefore, going solely on advice from others was confusing, because more often than not there were contradictions. I knew that the Bible shouldn't contradict itself, so I decided that I would have to study it out for myself.

Two: When I would ask advice from different ministers, I found that even ministers would have different opinions from other ministers. Because ministers are human just as we are, they too looked at the Bible through human eyes. This meant that there would be times that there would be opposing views. The Bible says that now we see through a glass darkly. This means that we will not understand everything on this side clearly. This applies to the ministry as well.

Three: When I would use Bible commentaries, I found that even the commentaries would not always agree. I realized that just because it was on paper and ink did not mean that it was automatically correct. Even published works detailing what the Bible meant to say needed to be taken with a grain of salt.

I am not trying to be judgemental, but as stated earlier, we are all human, and we will all see through a glass darkly. That is why it is so important to study the Bible for ourselves and not depend on a man solely for our nourishment. Individual time spent in reading and searching the Bible is vital to our spiritual growth.

Four: I found that symbolism was used a lot in the Bible and what the symbol meant varied from one view to the next. This symbolism, if interpreted the wrong way, could lead to incorrect views on the Bible.

Five: I found one part of the Bible was basically translated from Hebrew and Aramaic and another part was translated from Greek, and there were differences in the translations of the root words. This meant that there could be discrepancies if the Bible was not studied all the way back to its roots. We can't always attach one definition to a word. There are times when the translators used a single word to cover several different concepts.

Six: There were several translations of the Bible, and while the translators were to remain neutral, there is some discussion as to how well they were able to accomplish this. It would be human nature to apply the way you feel is right to the work that you are translating. Therefore, this could have led to translations that were not neutral in their approach. There could have been slanting at times towards a person's particular doctrinal view.

Seven: Probably the most troubling of all reasons about different views was how much "motive" was behind the interpretation of a scripture; i.e., someone using the Bible to promote their personal views for a personal reason. This is a dangerous approach. If used incorrectly and only in part, a person could justify sin in their life either intentionally or unintentionally. The Bible has to be taken in whole and not in part.

So how do I find a way to use this book properly? *How do I make sure that the right view comes out?* How do I make sure that I don't use my own opinions to "slant" the scriptures the way I like them? I spent a lot of time studying these questions for myself. I felt that the Bible was the guide to reach the goals that I wanted to reach, and I wanted to apply and study the scriptures correctly. I devised the following method for studying, and I would like to share that method with you. You can be the judge and decide if it is profitable for you.

Before I begin, I would like to clarify and explain my choice in Bible translations. I choose to use the King James Version as the primary version or translation, not because other translations are improper, but because this is all I knew for many years. Also, I feel most comfortable with the way the K.J.V. handles the language.

First, don't discard any scriptures. Paul writes in his second letter to Timothy, *"All scripture is given by inspiration of God."*[2]

In studying, I would find scriptures I did not like and did not understand. This is going to happen. There will be times that the scriptures are not clear to you. The answer is not to throw these scriptures away. If I throw out any scripture for any reason, I run the risk of altering the instruction in some way. This can be harmful. I understand that God did not ask me what scripture should or should not be in the Bible, so it is not up to me to decide what is and is not profitable. While I still don't understand every verse (in fact many), I do reread them at

---

[2] II Timothy 3:16

times to see if my understanding has changed. I have found that as I get closer to the Lord, the more the scriptures come alive in my mind. The key for me has been patience and study. I don't feel that discarding the scriptures will ever bring correct answers.

Second, consider context definitions. When definitions of words are in doubt, how do you settle on a definition? While there are scholars *translating and intellectuals* assigning definitions, I feel none of them are as smart as God. For example, Webster was a very smart man, but we cannot go to his dictionary to find the definitions to words in the Bible on every occasion. When I am in doubt about what a word means, I try to find a scripture in the Bible that states what the definition is. For example, if a scripture uses the term "God's love," I find a scripture that states what God's love is. I do not mean a scripture that says it is wonderful or great. While it is these things, I find a scripture that says what love means. For myself, I find that this method adds continuity to all scriptures.

Third, consider the translator's struggles. Consider the tone of the scripture, the environment it was written in, the environment that the translation took place under, all the information available to help the translators, and the lack of additional information that may have hindered the translation. I would suggest not reading more into the translation than is there. While we should not discard a scripture, I don't know if it is wise to "squeeze" a "round" scripture into a "square" hole. If at first we are not sure where a scripture fits, we can come back to it later. It is not necessary to understand the place of every scripture on the first read through of the Bible. This takes time and a lot of patience. We will never see everything on this side. We just have to do the best we can.

Fourth, all scriptures harmonize. God does not contradict himself, so if two passages seem to state the same subject differently, then going slow in an interpretation would be worth considering. It might help to look for additional scriptures that would better help them blend. It is imperative to remember that the Bible should be considered as the authority.

Fifth, scriptures should be interpreted literally first if possible. My experience is that when individuals use too much symbolism, it is very easy for motive to come into play. This results in people "using" the scriptures differently than intended. So if a symbol is used to support a literal view, I have found I can put more confidence in that view. It is a harder to support a view that is based solely on symbolism. I do not want to indicate symbols are not useful, but they have to be used carefully.

Here are few examples of symbolism:

"He shall cover thee with his feathers, and under his wings shalt thou trust: his truth shall be thy shield and buckler." (Psalm 91:4)

*"And God said, **Let us make man in our image**, after our likeness: and let them have dominion over the fish of the sea, and over the fowl of the air, and over the cattle, and over all the earth, and over every creeping thing that creepeth upon the earth." (Genesis 1:26)*

We know that as humans we have no feathers. This is a simple example of a symbol being used to describe the covering of God. Some symbols are more difficult to place.

Sixth, consider volume to value. If 25 scriptures handle a word or subject one way and 2 scriptures seem to handle it differently, what should we do? While we're not to throw away the 2 scriptures, we also should not throw away the 25 scriptures, because we like the 2 scriptures better. With time and study, the scriptures that do not "fit" will most of the time fall into the correct place.

Seventh, scripture is a higher authority than traditions. I do think that traditions have value. The Bible is full of traditions and some come with instructions that they should be kept. What should be done about traditions today that are not supported by the Bible? Believing what you think is in the Bible and believing what the Bible actually says may be totally different. Just because someone you have allowed to have influence in your life says something is in the Bible, this should not be enough. You should search it out for yourself. For example, most likely we have all heard someone say to us that "cleanliness is next to Godliness." While it is good to be clean, this is not a scripture that is in the Bible. It has been a tradition that has been quoted from generation to generation. While this is a simple example, there are some traditions that may conflict with God's word. It is our responsibility to search the scriptures out. (Note: This is much easier today with the aide of computers.)

In conclusion, it is important to study the Bible for ourselves. It takes time and patience. These are just a few of the things that I have applied to my study of the scriptures. As stated earlier, you be the judge if they are profitable. It all comes down to an individual study of the scripture. Think of the word of God like a river. If you go to the source of the river, it is the purest that you will find the water. The farther down the stream you go, the more polluted the water will become. This is how we should study the scripture. While it is not wrong to go to ministers, use commentaries or study aids, the purest source that we will find when trying to know more about God is His Word. The Bible is the purest source that we can access.

Chapter 5

Finding Peace over Hell

After dealing with the anger and pride in my life, another area of concern that was very troubling was whether I would go to hell or not. (I believed I had already been to hell.) There are a lot of scriptures covering this subject in the Bible, so I wanted to make sure that I had a clear understanding of this subject. I had heard of hell from people around me, and I wanted to know if I would have to go there one day.

My parents would visit many different types of churches, and of course if my parents went to church, that meant the children would be going also. This was not an option when I was a child. In visiting these different churches, I was exposed very early in my life to many different concepts.

One type of sermon would always seem to get my attention above the others. This was a sermon about fire and brimstone. The message always seemed to be, "Hell is hot, and you're going to pop and fry for eternity." I would sit in the pew almost frozen with fear as the minister blasted this sermon over the pulpit. Hearing the terms and description of this place called hell was not pleasant for me. I don't want to come across as a know it all, but I felt like because of my burns I had sufficient understanding of what it meant to "pop and fry." I knew what it felt like to burn.

Some nights as a boy, I would not be able to sleep from the fear of hell. I would toss and turn, because I would be shaking with fear about some hell-fire sermon. Other nights, I might get some sleep but would have horrible nightmares in which something was going to hurt me. The thought of hell brought me torment when I was a child. For many years, I just tried to live with these emotions the best way that I could. For a while, I learned to live with the blazing fear that being sent to hell caused me.

      One thing I did not understand as a child was the lack of emotion in others around me. I did not understand why others listening to the same sermons did not seem to have the same reaction I did. While I was losing sleep at night from fear, they seemed to brush off the subject without a care in the world. They sat in the same pews that I did and listened to the same hellfire sermons I did but seemed cavalier in their response to the minister pouring his heart into these sermons. They were meant to scare us into submission, and for me this was the result. While it sparked a reaction in my life, many others around me seemed to take hell lightly. Where was their fear? Where was their seriousness? Didn't they know how horrible "popping and frying" for eternity would be?

Finally, after finding some success with my anger and pride by using the Bible as my guide, I got up the courage to do a complete study of hell from the Bible. Over forty years ago, we did not have all the electronic aids that we have today. We had no computers or computer programs to lean on. These days, you can type in a word, and a computer program will print out every reference in the entire Bible in which this word is used. We did not have this luxury when I was a child. Therefore, I made this study of hell the best I could.

Because our family had Bible reading on a regular basis, I had access to several resources in my home. My parents called our family devotional time "Bible reading." We also had several Bibles and several different types of concordances. One was a "complete" concordance and another was a "comprehensive" concordance. We had several smaller versions, so I used these as a starting point for my study.

To begin with, I wanted to know for sure what this horrible place called hell was going to be like. I took a legal pad and listed every scriptural reference on hell from one concordance. Then, I took all the other concordances and listed any scripture reference on hell that the first concordance had left out. I listed every scripture that I could find in these notebooks. I also found that in the translation process, there had been different root words used, like Hades, Sheol, grave, Gehenna, and even Tartaro. I looked up all the root words in the concordance and added those scriptural references to the list on the subject of hell.

Next, I took my Bible and my list and wrote out long hand every scriptural passage on the list. This effort consumed several legal pads and many, many hours of labor on just this one subject. After I had the scriptures penned down, I would take the written out scriptures on the list and read them over and over. It was made easier by having them readily available without having to flip through the Bible each time. I read over this subject of hell more times than I can remember. I know all of this sounds like a lot for a boy to do, but my experience of actually being burned drove me to complete this task. I had a fear in my heart of hell, and I instinctively knew, even as a boy, that the study of the subject would help me find peace. I had been to "hell" and didn't ever want to go there again.

    I began to ask different people their opinion of hell. As you can imagine, I got a lot of different answers. Some of the answers seemed thoughtful. They seemed genuinely concerned about living in a way that would prevent them from experiencing hell first hand. Others were more flippant. I have found that with some people, if it is out of sight, it is out of mind. They blew off the subject, because it was not something that was going to happen in the near future. It was not as real to them as it was to me.

    What I found most often is that few grownups had ever studied the subject of hell as in-depth as I had as a child. No one appeared to be serious or concerned about the popping and frying sermons. Even with all the scripture available in the Bible, it did not seem to be a priority to people. They did not appear to have the fear that I had. Even as a child, I did not understand why such a serious subject was not studied more.

I did not realize it at the time, but I was observing human emotion struggling with the Bible. My parents, my pastors, my elders, and other ministers struggled emotionally with the reality of hell as an eternal destination. They seemed to deal with this subject in general terms, always avoiding detailed discussions of hell. They talked a lot in generalizations of hell but spoke little specifics. As I came to understand, it is human nature to avoid a subject that we do not find pleasant. It is easy to study the Bible and find scriptures on God's love, but it is not very easy or pleasant to dwell on the scriptures that deal with God's judgement.

Even as a young boy, this was an extremely serious subject for me. I do feel that being burned made me look at the subject of hell more seriously. For me, it was more like I was a veteran from a war. When a veteran hears rumors of going to war, it brings back the images of what he experienced. He sees the death, destruction, and sorrow that war can bring. He relives the experience of being on the battlefield. He sees, smells, and hears the war. All of his senses are engaged. The idea of war for him is more tangible. He has a deeper concern when hearing of going to war. Whereas someone who has never been to war only knows the concept of war and not the harsh reality of it. It is not as real to those who have never been on the battlefield. Therefore it is easier to brush it off rather lightly. This is where I was. I had been burned. I had smelled my own flesh burning. I had felt the panic and fear of "hell" here on earth, so for me, it was a bigger concern than for others, and I knew that whatever outcome my studies might bring, I still wanted to know all of the details. I wanted to know what was coming.

Now, I do not mind discussing this subject, and I no longer have the fears that I had as a child. Even though I have peace with this subject, I feel that, because of the seriousness of hell, each person should do an in-depth study, especially if they need to find the same inner peace that I had sought for myself.

In the course of your own study, you will probably find that there are many different opinions, and that will bring up the issue of who to believe. For me, I've found comfort in finding my answers in the pages of the Bible itself. I decided fairly early that I could trust the Bible more than any other source of instruction.

I will share one passage from scripture concerning hell that was very helpful to me.

"**And death and hell were cast into the lake of fire.** This is the second death." (Rev. 20:14)

This one passage from the Bible helped me separate the study of hell from the study of the "lake of fire." It helped me to realize that whatever hell was, it was **not** the lake of fire. This scripture very clearly puts a separation between the two. If hell is the lake of fire, how can you throw something into itself?

This in-depth study of hell brought me more peace than any other method I had tried. Talking with my elders, reading commentaries, and using aids did not bring the peace that my own personal study had brought me. While I used this technique for my study of hell, this process can be applied to any area of our lives. Studying the Bible for my primary source is a method that I've found works best for me. If you desire to have peace over some type of hell in your life, I would suggest that you read and study the Bible over and over until you've found that peace. The word of God is like a well of living water. It is continual exposure to this well of water that brings peace to our life. You cannot depend solely on others around you for understanding of the Bible. To find true peace, you have to walk your own journey through the scriptures. My experience with studying the Bible has elevated the value of the Bible. The more I study, the more "life" and peace I find in its pages. Every time I read through the Bible, the Lord opens up something new to me that I did not see before. It is truly a living well that never runs dry!

    To clarify, I do not mean that other resources should not be used. The question that arises is how profitable would it be to only read books about the Bible. How wise is it to not go to the source? Would not the water be purest at the beginning instead of after flowing over dirt, rubble, and shifting sand way down stream? I found in my studies that the Bible is a good test for testing the validity of other resources. The Ephesian church was commended in the book of Revelation for trying or testing those who said they were apostles and finding them to be liars. We should not just accept without question any source other than the Bible. We should study out and test to see if what we are reading or hearing is true. Even the things that I have said thus far, I would encourage you to test for yourself; read and study the Bible to see how profitable my methods are for you.

My conclusion over the study of hell is that you should use your Bible, begin your own journey, and find your own personal peace.

Chapter 6

External Peace vs. Internal Peace

Even when considering the very words external and internal creates two very different focused areas of concern. While it is easy to recognize the difference between external and internal peace, the real difficulty comes in determining how each one affects the other. There were many factors that contributed to what I felt was a lack of peace in my own life. It was not solely what I was going through internally, the environment that I lived in also affected how I was coping with my internal struggle. One major factor that contributed to my lack of internal peace was the external condition of finances. Although I was only a boy, I realized what a struggle finances were in our home. Even before the medical bills from my burns, my family lived on a rather limited income.

My medical procedures were extensive, and health insurance coverage for me was limited. Insurance to cover my all my hospital procedures was not something we could depend on for everything I needed. During that period of time, there were very few burn victims that had survived the degree of burn that I had endured. The treatments that I needed were often considered experimental. My procedures were sometimes funded in different ways. I still remember having doctors and those investing their funds into the doctors' work, crowded in my examination room at the same time. The doctors would point out what and how they had done certain procedures. The committees funding the surgeries would then ask questions. These questions were not in regard to my health and well being. They were simply questioning the medical techniques that were used to achieve particular results.

Because I lived in a very small country town, most of these procedures were in locations that were far from where we lived. We did not have access to funds for commercial flights. We also did not always have a vehicle that was dependable enough to make long road trips. I remember my mother flagging down a Greyhound or Trailway bus along side the road, so we could start on a journey for another medical procedure. I've slept many hours on buses going to and from hospitals and clinics. I remember once being in a large city and my mother "splurging" on a store-bought hamburger for ten cents. She would sleep on cots in my hospital rooms where I waited for and recovered from various surgeries. Money was very tight for us then.

It would certainly have been easier for me then if my parents had had access to more money. All those trips would have surely been more comfortable. I would not have had to worry at all about the burden those medical bills caused my family. I would have had a lot less external stress if this would have been the case. In my opinion, it is completely normal to think that a nicer environment would have made me feel better. I'm not saying that external peace will not have any effect on us. I am saying that my goal is to have internal peace, but the idea that our external circumstances will never affect how we feel internally is absolutely false.

    I regularly pray and ask God for help. Prayer is one of the most important things I do to have internal peace. When I was a boy, a minister at a church I attended suggested to me that I sought God too much. His advice was confusing to me as a child, because I felt like I didn't have any choice but to seek God. I knew that I wanted peace, comfort, and inner strength, and the only source for these things was God. I still believe that you cannot seek God too much. He is our source of strength. He wants us to come to Him with our struggles. My goal of internal peace was one that I felt was worthwhile. I could not be content where I was internally; there was still too much anger. Anger, pride, and all these struggles seemed to interfere with what I desired. I had tried in my own strength to take care of my problems, but all I did was fail miserably. This helped me realize the only way to achieve the end result that I wanted was through a relationship with God.

One passage from the Bible that I have used in this area is Exodus 16:4: *"Then said the LORD unto Moses, Behold, I will rain **bread from heaven** for you; and the people shall **go out and gather a certain rate every day**, that I may prove them, whether they will walk in my law, or no."*

Even in my childhood, I understood that, like the garden my mother put out every year that I was "blessed" to work in, if you let the weeds go too long you've lost the garden for that year. This is a natural example that has a very profitable spiritual application. Let me explain.

In gardening, you have to weed the garden every day or two. If not, the weeds get out of control and overtake what you've planted. Just like weeding the garden regularly, I learned to try to work on my struggles on a regular basis and avoid letting them go until they consumed me.

This passage also helped me seek God every day for bread from heaven. The Israelites of the Exodus were commanded to get fresh manna every day or else the manna would rot. We have to seek God and receive from him daily in order to stay healthy in our walk with the Lord. This is not to say that it will always be pleasant. It is a little dry at times, but so is flour. You just have to learn how to work the flour into a more pleasant form.

In continually dealing with my internal, as well as my external struggles, I often tried to handle them in my own way. Even in my late teens, I had become a "list" person. I set goals. I set daily goals, weekly goals, and even yearly goals. Some I wrote down, and some I memorized. In regards to my internal peace, I began to set external goals, trying to make the environment around me a better place to live, while setting internal goals in order to come to a place where I had peace with myself and God.

Everything was settled then, and I was ready to put my life on automatic. My goals had been set, so my problems were settled! What a joke that turned out to be. As I tried to work from my list, I realized what an extensive job it would be. I was not going to be able to just check my struggles off a list. For example, although I was grateful that my problem with anger had been identified, I was still reminded from time to time that the anger had not gone away completely. It was not something that I could check off my weekly-goals list. It took time to deal with each different area.

I also found that every time it seemed like I had gotten a problem under control, something new would rear up. I realize now that most of my difficulties were already there, but I was not able to see them. I was busy with some other problems. This is a blessing looking back. The Lord seems to allow us to see only parts of our nature at a time. We would be overwhelmed if he just let us see everything we needed to work on at one time. He knows what we are able to bear.

Usually there seemed to be some external problem as well as some internal problem battling in me at the same time. Sometimes, these problems seemed to be polar opposites; there seemed to be no relationship between the two whatsoever.

I tried working on the external, so life would be more comfortable. Growing up, I walked a lot. I walked to the store for mother to get her grocery items. One place we lived, it was a quarter of a mile to the store. Another place, it was one mile each way to the store. We would walk to the store and walk to the river to go fishing which was one to two miles away. As children, we did not have all of the electronic toys that kids have today. We devised our toys and play with the things that were around us. A lot of our childhood games involved walking miles in the woods looking for animal tracks or checking out a swimming hole. All this walking was good for us as children. It helped keep us strong and healthy, but it was still a lot of walking. When I finally got to use a bicycle, life became much easier. Much less walking meant I could check walking off my list of external factors to relieve. When I got to ride in a car, it was even easier than that, but when the car had air conditioning, my life was even more comfortable.

I remember my father buying a brand new car without air conditioning, because it was supposed to get two to three miles per gallon more. At that time, gas was twenty-five cents a gallon. Even air conditioning was not a luxury that was always a factor in our childhood.

I began to learn there were a lot more "comforts" that I wanted to enjoy. The challenge of trying to make my immediate external environment more comfortable was a never-ending effort. While I appreciate outside comforts, they can become a stumbling block. With my efforts to make my external circumstances more palatable, I have found a problem involving the following scripture:

*"Hell and destruction are never full; so **the eyes of man are never satisfied.**" (Prov. 27:20)*

I'd like to share some thoughts on fixing the external. To clarify before I begin, if you're looking for advice on how to live a "righteous" life in order to be materially rich, I'm not the one to give it. While I appreciate the natural blessings I have received in my life, I feel the main focus is to understand the internal peace He offers. Our goal should not be to simply live as comfortably as we can. I realize the external affects us, but it must be considered very carefully.

First off, I have been exposed to some areas of thought through seminars and books about the power of positive thinking, goal setting, and planning your work and working your plan. While there is some validity in these thoughts, they cannot be relied on solely. I am old enough now to have had some natural successes. Even in these natural successes, there have been times that I have done everything that I could have done and worked very hard and still had natural failures. This will happen at times.

On the natural side, I would like to point out that I have grown to appreciate being born in a society that allows freedom of movement, freedom of land ownership, and freedom of speech. There are many great things I have been able to enjoy just because of where I was born. This is one area that my external circumstances have affected me.

Secondly, some areas that trouble me are the ways that individuals or institutions try to use religion to handle natural concepts. One example of this is when religious leaders tie natural success to spiritual success. I have heard it promoted that the richer you are, the more favored by God you must be. This is not a scriptural doctrine. It is only normal for a person trying to have a positive relationship with the Lord to listen to others that claim to have that same desire. Over the years, I have perceived that at times a "slant" is put on Bible scriptures for some other purpose than what God intended. A serious study of the Bible is to be just that, "serious." When we "share" a concept, we should take responsibility to try to share it exactly like the Lord meant it to be shared.

It's normal to like the stories of natural success found in the Bible like Daniel and the lion's den and the three Hebrew children in the fiery furnace. There are many stories that end with natural success. You also have to consider the parts of the Bible that seem to imply a humble natural setting and a Godly blessing at the same time.

For example in Ecclesiastes 9:15 it states, *"Now there was found in it a poor wise man, and he by his wisdom delivered the city; yet no man remembered that same poor man."*

The fact that the man was poor and wise would be contraindicative to some lines of thought.

Thirdly, another area that is troubling is an area that I call implication teaching instead of relying on solid concepts. One uses an implication that has some questionable motive or intent in it. They do not use solid scriptural principles; they twist scriptures to imply something that they want to use to their benefit in some way. The sad part is when someone follows what they think is solid Christian advice and fails. (When it does not work for them, that person can become even more discouraged and confused.) This can cause these people to lose the good that God wants them to have.

This is found in the religious world quite often. Leaders promote the concept that a natural blessing is a sign of God's favor. For example, a Christian with a nicer automobile, a nicer home, and a bigger bank account means that he has found favor with God. Some would even go as far as to say that God loves them more than the poor Christian. Others often promote health as a sign of God's favor. They say that the Christian who enjoys good health is a better Christian than the individual struggling with health issues.

Another thought promotes that knowledge and education are ways to find more favor with God. It is very disturbing to hear the doctrine promoted that "smart" people are more blessed or have more favor with God than those who struggle with the ability to learn. Where did these individuals that are classified as "smart" get their abilities from? Did they work hard from the beginning of their educational start, or are genetics involved? This is all a part of the creation process. Some are born with different abilities, but those abilities are still all God given. There is nothing that is done to deserve the abilities we may or may not have. You cannot elevate a person that is considered smart above a person that is challenged intellectually. In reality, when in comparison to God, we are all challenged intellectually!

I guess you could ask the question. "Who would want to be associated with a loser?" Some think that when we live to have the Lord in our lives that it's all about being a winner. We must be careful, because when Jesus was hanging on a cross, He did not look like a winner.

I think that it's necessary to look past the outside to find success in the Lord regardless of what our circumstances are. No matter what station we might find ourself in life, we all have the same opportunities handed to us by God. We all have the opportunity to accept what God is handing out to us if we are willing to serve Him. I want that inner peace and have had to learn that the outside environment can be deceiving. I do not want to be distracted from searching for the inner peace from God by always being concerned about the external "blessings."

I have noticed that even when natural success happens God's way, this natural side is not as important as the proper relationship with God. When this natural success becomes our sole focus, it can cause us to drift in our relationship with the Lord. We all have to live in this natural world, but we just have to remember that our goal is to have a good relationship with the Lord.

*"And when Herod would have brought him forth, **the same night Peter was sleeping between two soldiers**, bound with two chains: and the keepers before the door kept the prison."* (Acts 12:6)

Here was the Apostle Peter knowing that the next day he might be executed, but he was sound asleep. (Due process of law was a "little" different under the Roman Empire.) He had peace with whatever the outcome might have been. I have to admit that if I knew I was going to die the next day, I might have a little trouble sleeping. Even though the account ends with the natural success, it does not mean it could have been otherwise. Having peace with God in the middle of trying times is a powerful thought to me.

*"And when he had opened the fifth seal, **I saw under the altar the souls of them that were slain for the word of God**, and for the testimony which they held…"* (Rev. 6:9)

Telling people they might die for their faith is not the best way to win souls for Christ, but understanding that in the face of difficult circumstances regardless of what is going on externally, we can have inner peace with God brings a level of spiritual success that does not come from focusing solely on the natural.

There have been times in my life when it seemed that I had troubles on every side. But, even in the midst of the worst storm, there is an inner peace that you can have if you have a good relationship with the Lord.

Chapter 7

Vision for the Future

Going back to the time in my life when I was wrestling with popping and frying in hell, I began to study not only how to live successfully in this world spiritually but also on what comes after this life. I began to think of this very young, because I realized that I was very close to dying during that period of my life. It was used as a tool of encouragement by those around me. They felt like I should be reminded of how wonderful it was that God saved me and kept me from dying that day. At a very young age, this created questions in my heart about my eternal future.

Through the years, I gradually began to develop a grudging thankfulness for what I perceived as God's interest in me. I still struggled with anger, pride, and other areas, but I began to appreciate God. The questions that I had about what was to come for me still lingered in my mind. I was steadily dealing with the present, but I also began to see the need to prepare for the future. I began to understand that the future would come, whether it was simply in this world or in God's eternal plan. I began to seek God and question about this "future."

At first, I took these questions to my elders and peers. As usual, I got a variety of responses. Each person would explain heaven to me in a different way. One person told me that it was a place without pain. I liked that idea because I knew even at that young age what pain was all about. I enjoyed the idea of a future with no more suffering. I also received the response that I would be with Jesus all the time. As a child, I wasn't sure what that meant and why it was supposed to be good to be with Jesus. At that point in my life, he was still just a character in a story in a book. I had never met Him, so it really was not important to me to be able to spend all my time with Him. Another explanation was that I would be with my family and friends who had already passed away. As a child, I had not really been close to any one in my family or social circle who passed away. The idea of heaven just being a place to see these unfamiliar people again did not really appeal to me either. I knew that Heaven was described as a wonderful place, but I did not understand fully why. The concept of heaven as a great place to end up, to be with Jesus forever, and to see all those I had known at one time who had already died was very confusing to me.

Once when I was still just a boy, I remember seeing a big picture or painting on the wall of a church. It had a clear, sky blue background and what appeared to be a big, white, fluffy cloud. Sitting in the middle of this cloud was a child approximately 10 to 12 years old wearing a white robe and playing a harp. Since it was in the church, I assumed that it must have been important somehow. When I asked what the picture was supposed to mean, I got the most puzzling answer. The person, who was trying to help me understand, stated that it represented heaven. I was completely confused by this idea. I felt through my earlier experiences that I had already had enough of "hell," but this picture of heaven was not as appealing as I thought it should be. At that place in my life, if it would have shown a boy with his legs hanging over the edge of the cloud holding a fishing pole, I probably would have been a bit more interested. You can see that at this point in my life I was very puzzled by the concept of heaven. I did not want hell, but heaven did not seem very interesting either. I knew that there must be more to the story, so I began to search out the answer I was seeking. What was heaven really like?

      This study was a very slow process. Just like the study of hell, the study of heaven has many views. Some feel that almost everyone should go to heaven, leaving the need of hell in question. Some feel that almost everyone should go to hell, making heaven seem like quite a lonesome place. I knew that there must be more, so I began my journey once more; this time in quest of heaven, whatever that might be.

The idea of heaven at times is hard to understand, because everyone wants to say their loved ones will be there. It is incredibly upsetting to think of those we love not making it into heaven. Other times, there are people that are ready to send someone to hell the minute after they do something to upset them. It seems to be easy when emotions are running high to want to use the Bible as a whip against your enemies. While this is our first human instinct, it is not what God wants. The Bible says that we have to love our enemies. Sending them to "hell" is not an example of love. It is easy to see why this subject is so very touchy. It is emotional for most people to deal with, because it touches every person in our lives.

All of this confusion was one reason that I sought answers from the Lord through the Bible. I knew that if I could find inner peace with God, that inevitably I would have a better future. This gave me hope. Although the confusion was overwhelming at times, I tried not to lose sight of the goal that I had. I knew in my heart that I would have a better tomorrow if I just trusted and sought God today.

This subject was not one that I dealt with and put away forever. It was not as black and white for me as it seemed to be for some people. As I dealt with different issues and emotions in my life, I would come back time and time again to wondering what God's overall plan was for the future.

As time went by, the picture of the boy playing the harp on a cloud did not come into mind much. Different experiences began to shape my life, and I began to feel like I was "traveling" through life. I had some successes and some failures, and gradually I tried to learn from these experiences.

What did the future hold? There was my earthly or natural "future" before I was to die. This is the question of how I would live my life on the earth before my time came to die. There was also the question of my heavenly "future" after I was to die. What came after this life?

Even though I was young, I knew I had come close to dying. Because death was so real to me on a personal level, I did not like to be reminded that death was coming. In reading my Bible, though, I was continually reminded.

The scriptures are a manual of how not only to live my life in this world, but also how to grow closer to the Lord in order to be ready for what is to come after my time on this earth is officially over. The following passage helped me to understand just how fleeting life could be:

"Whereas ye know not what shall be on the morrow. For what is your life? It is even a vapour, that appeareth for a little time, and then vanisheth away." (James 4:14)

I knew my life had been drastically altered in just the few seconds it took to be burned; it was not hard to realize life could end the same way.

Besides my burn, I had learned very young how quickly death could come. When I was about 12, a neighbor boy and I were playing marbles in the yard. We were having fun and enjoying the day. Just a few minutes later, my mother called me to come in and get ready to go. We had planned to visit a family ten miles away. We finished our game, and I left with my family to visit our friends. While we were visiting this family, a dreadful phone call came. They told us that my friend who I been playing marbles with just a few hours earlier had been hit by a car and killed. Life can end in just a moment. There are no guarantees! Our life truly is a vapor.

Understanding how fleeting life can be should help us all to realize what our focus should be. Should it be on the natural? Should gaining earthly riches be our primary goal? It is important to realize that all natural successes end at the grave. No matter what we achieve naturally, we can't stop the process of death. Even with this knowledge, there are still some that try to find a way to hold death at bay. How long have men been looking for the fountain of youth?

While I considered the immediate future because of issues that seemed to be closer, I also began to study the Bible about the future waiting for us after death.

Just as I did a serious study of the subject of hell, I also began a serious study of the life after death. This study did have a different approach. For my study of hell, I had approached it very singularly and focused, but my study of "heaven" took on a broader method.

There were words that seemed to be describing another place, but I could not be sure they were describing the same place. I'd like to share a short list of scriptures which I consider that all are trying to describe life after this current existence. To me all these scriptures seem to be in the future. You can decide for yourself if they have ever been accomplished on this earth.

"I saw in the night visions, and, behold, one like the Son of man came with the clouds of heaven, and came to the Ancient of days, and they brought him near before him. And there was given him dominion, and glory, and a kingdom, that all people, nations, and languages, should serve him: his dominion is an everlasting dominion, which shall not pass away, and his kingdom that which shall not be destroyed." (Daniel 7:13)

This scripture seems to describe what we will be a part of if we get to be there. It describes a kingdom in which every creature will be a servant of God. Looking around at this world, it is clear that this has not been accomplished yet.

"And there shall come forth a rod out of the stem of Jesse, and a Branch shall grow out of his roots: And the spirit of the LORD shall rest upon him, the spirit of wisdom and understanding, the spirit of counsel and might, the spirit of knowledge and of the fear of the LORD; And shall make him of quick understanding in the fear of the LORD: and he shall not judge after the sight of his eyes, neither reprove after the hearing of his ears: But **with righteousness shall he judge** the poor, and reprove with equity for the meek of the earth: and he shall smite the earth with the rod of his mouth, and with the breath of his lips shall he slay the wicked. And righteousness shall be the girdle of his loins, and faithfulness the girdle of his reins. The wolf also shall dwell with the lamb, and the leopard shall lie down with the kid; and the calf and the young lion and the fatling together; and a little child shall lead them. And the cow and the bear shall feed; their young ones shall lie down together: and the **lion shall eat straw like the ox**. **And the sucking child shall play on the hole of the asp, and the weaned child shall put his hand on the cockatrice' den.** They shall not hurt nor destroy in all my holy mountain: for the earth shall be full of the knowledge of the LORD, as the waters cover the sea. And in that day there shall be a root of Jesse, which shall stand for an ensign *of the people; to it shall the Gentiles seek: and his rest shall be glorious." (Isaiah 11:1-10)*

"And in that day will I make a covenant for them with the beasts of the field, *and with the fowls of heaven, and with the creeping things of the ground:* **and I will break the bow and the sword and the battle out of the earth, and will make them to lie down safely."** *(Hosea 2:18)*

Just as it happened in the days after Noah and the flood, these passages describe a land where even the very laws of nature have changed. A child can play with a snake, and a lion shall eat straw like an ox. This describes a place where there is no more violence. It is a land of peace. There seems to be no fear in this place.

"And the seventh angel sounded; and there were great voices in heaven, saying, The kingdoms of this world are become the kingdoms

of our Lord, and of his Christ; and he shall reign for ever and ever." (Revelation 11:15)

Some people teach the doctrine that this world will go out of existence after the Lord returns. This scripture seems to imply that the world will in fact still remain. The difference will be that there is going to be a righteous government.

*"**He answered and said unto them, Because it is given unto you to know the mysteries of the kingdom of heaven**, but to them it is not given." (Matthew 13:11)*

*"**And I saw a new heaven and a new earth**: for the first heaven and the first earth were passed away; and there was no more sea." (Revelation 21:1)*

Could part of the changes coming simply be that we will be able to "see" more? Will we be able to understand the workings of God's realm more than we do now? II Kings 6:17 states, *"And Elisha prayed, and said, LORD, I pray thee, open his eyes, that he may see. And the LORD opened the eyes of the young man; and he saw: and, behold, the mountain was full of horses and chariots of fire round about Elisha."* The horses and chariots were there the entire time; Elisha's helper just could not see them.

"Jesus answered and said unto him, If a man love me, he will keep my words: and my Father will love him, and **we will come** *unto him,* **and make our abode with him.***" (John 14:23)*

"In my Father's house are many mansions: *if it were not so, I would have told you. I go to prepare a place for you." (John 14:2)*

"There are also celestial bodies, and bodies terrestrial: *but the glory of the celestial is one, and the glory of the terrestrial is another. There is one glory of the sun, and another glory of the moon, and another glory of the stars: for one star differeth from another star in glory.* ***So also is the resurrection of the dead.*** *It is sown in corruption; it is raised in incorruption:" (I Corinthians 15:40)*

These scriptures all deal with us dwelling in that new place. They also deal with the type of body that we will have when we finally reach the place that God has for us. I have to admit that having a celestial body seems very special, especially compared to the beat-up, scarred-up, old, worn-out body that I have now.

This short list discusses many thoughts about life in God's plan for us. In searching out the Bible, you will find that there are many, many other references that deal with the promises of God. In my studies, I began to sense that there was a "greatness" that the Lord was holding out to us.

I have come through many things in my life, some of them quite traumatic and very difficult, yet I appreciate all the good things God has helped me with. I have found that this is a key to success in God. While it is profitable for us to look back at the lessons we have learned, we must also look forward in hope with the understanding that our future is so very bright.

What is one hundred years here-and-now compared to an eternity of being part of God's plan?

If God's plan holds out the prospect of receiving a celestial body, what natural reward could compare?

For me, although I truly feel like I started in hell, the more I understand the "promises" of God, the brighter my hope and vision in the Lord becomes.